Praise for *The Called Home Novella*

This book, *The Called Home Novella* was absolutely life changing. I love reading anything that Dianne Congdon writes. The love of Jesus absolutely writes through her. God has anointed her in such amazing ways. I cried several times while I read this book. Dianne poured her heart out through every single page to offer anyone the love and support they might need during a time of preparing of losing a loved one. I also believe that this book would help prepare any person going through any form of grief. I know there are many ways that a person can grieve. Dianne shows us, by her example in each story she shares, of how to love and let go and how to prepare to do this.

I loved how this book was written in a devotional format and it helped me process one day at a time. Each day was so beautifully written as if I was right there experiencing what she went through at the time. I shed many tears and I had laughter and joy through reading different parts of the book as well. I am so overjoyed to be able to know Dianne personally. She truly lives her life for Jesus day in and day out. The love of Jesus absolutely shines through her. I have been forever changed by knowing her and reading this book. I pray you feel the love of Jesus and his arms wrapped around you as well while reading each word on every page. God bless you.

—**Missy Simms**

My Reflection

Sharing my heart may touch yours to answer the call for a deep and needed healing. My journey helped bring new life to my marriage with a deeper spiritual understanding. God showed me how to shift myself for my partner's relationship with the Lord. He Favored me in the calming of my heavy heart with victory through Him. Finally, the Lord has moved me to share ideas and insights, not to hide from the deep regrets but to embrace them with trust and faith in Him. My beloved was Called Home May 2021.

Other Books:

The Astonishing Joy Novella. The Recipe Novella—DonationOnly
The closer we walk, the greater the Joy!

Dianne's Websites:

www.IgniteJoyToday.com
www.YouthfulAgingLifetyle.com

"May the LORD Bless and Keep you; The LORD make his face shine on you. And be gracious to you; the LORD turn His Face toward you and give you peace."

—Numbers 6: 24-26

ABIDING in Him,
Dianne

The Called Home Novella

A Book of Tears -

Comfort in a Time of Grief

Dianne Congdon

Requests for information should be addressed to:
Dianne Congdon: Dianne@IgniteJoyToday.com

DEDICATION

*To the Person of the Holy Spirit
who fills me with Hope and Joy*

and

To my Beloved Husband, Bob

*and to our Children:
Abby, Bill, John, and Sheila.*

Contents

MY STORY

It was August in the year of COVID that I had my first tears. No one was going anywhere. No one came to visit. March mandates appeared one day and soon turned in weeks, then months, and by August, we were all ready for something. Bob had not been feeling well. Our personal lockdown started the year before, 2019. It started one day with never getting dressed, just comfy in his robe.

The Everglades Celebration Entertainment committee pulled together a music event. Freddie, the DJ, was our featured entertainer! Playing from his balcony on the 14th floor at Sky Harbor which faced our condo patio area, he had great country songs, patriotic tunes, and oldies but goodies! Those of us who lived on the pool deck level remained on our patios while others stepped out to shout from their balconies. Freddie did us proud! He had gathered us once before on the 4th of July for the first time to play music to forget the cares of COVID thinking.

Bob just happened to have one of those robe days. "What the heck?" I said, "Let's just go sit on our patio and take in the festivities." Well, then the couple slow dance music started—you remember, the quiet kind. Now, it seems long ago. Something in me beckoned to ask Bob to dance. There, in his robe and LLB fuzzy slippers, we stepped onto the patio. He took me in his arms, and slowly we moved. Suddenly the tears came as I became aware this would probably never happen again like this. It was such a tender moment witnessed by everyone. They clapped when we finished. That moment is forever a heart memory. My first tears had started.

You see, the Lord has the Holy Spirit holding the baton to orchestrate our lives. He knew it would be a moment to remember. You are having them as well. Listen to me. Capture them all.

Remember, what is planted in your heart will be with you forever. As I write this, seven months later, the same tears are emerging. God collects our tears because each one is a book, a story, and most of all, His Glory.

"You keep track of all my sorrows; you have collected my tears in your bottle."
—Psalm 56:8 (TPT)

A BOOK OF TEARS

THE GLORY GATES

MARCH 3RD

Have you ever had to return something from Amazon? Then you know it means going online to select your item and where to return it. Simple, right? I ordered this kitchen rug which turned out to be nothing as expected, so I just decided to send it back—no problem selecting the item. Selecting where to return it was more complicated.

Now, UPS is closest to me even though I had to pay a bit, so I checked that among the other choices, Whole Foods and Kohl's Department Stores. Kohl's was a reasonably long way away, so I naturally went with UPS out of convenience. I clicked on UPS, but Kohl's got checked. Now, how did this happen? I logged off and entered once again to try to change it. Nope! Taking a chance, I printed out the label clearly saying Kohl's for return and headed off to UPS. Foolish girl, am I. Of course, the lady says this has Kohl's insert on it and no, you cannot return here. It finally dawned on me God wanted me to go to Kohl's. Now, that caught my attention.

The next day, after making sure Bob was feeling well, off to Kohl's I went. Amazon returns were on the second floor. Without an issue I easily got my package up the elevator. Taking a left and a left, the lady said, you will find the Amazon station. Well, well, here it was right in the middle of Home Goods. Of course, I know why they have these stations, because you are captive now in Home Goods, working your way out with an instant return slip offering a discount to buy things. I took my time to wander and shop around. Bingo! Soon, I found the perfect gray outdoor mat that just fit the bill. I said, "Now, Lord, is there anything else for me?" It was then the "Gates" showed up on the wall of decorative pieces. My goodness! The Lord knew I wanted a decorative trim for my "Power Kitchen" window. Could this be the reason??? I picked one of them up, and wow, they were heavy and beautifully scrolled with wood trim to match my desk! I checked out the size and thought it best to make sure they would fit.

Getting home, I immediately measured, and they were beyond perfect. All night I dreamed of these "Glory Gates" which would complete my "Sacred Space!" The first thing the following day, after making sure Bob was in a good place, I went back, and of course, they were still there. An hour later, I had them secured to my window and immediately felt the Presence of the Lord as Heaven's Gates were before me. It would be only months later, and I learned I had created my "Spiritual Altar." A Family Spiritual Altar is a place where you come to talk with the Father. It is an intimate place of exchange. You may recall when Noah finally got off the Ark, the first thing he did was to build an Altar to have a platform to talk with God. My Altar, like Noah's Altar, is where I meet with my Heavenly Father, His Holy Spirit, and His Son, Yeshua. A lovely, scented candle glows beside me offering reassurance of God's Presence and Light in my life.

So, see, sometimes when your plans are interrupted, it is not a bother but a blessing. The Lord just took me to shed tears of Joy as I kept looking at my "Glory Gates." I treasure them most of all because they are a gift to me by obedience. Sacrifice bears a gift and obedience matters.

My friends, regard all things as bearers of gifts from the One who loves you most. Quickly, turn away from frustration to see the Lord is directing your steps.

Recall a situation where you did not follow your intuition only to learn it cost you time and effort instead.

"In their hearts, humans plan their course, but the Lord established their steps."
—Proverbs 16:9 (NIV)

LISTEN WITH YOUR HEART

MARCH 6TH

Finally, after much delay, I began watching "The James Goll Mentoring Series," *Discerning the Times and the Seasons 2021.* So many valuable sessions already given were waiting for me. I am not good with a lot of loose ends. SO, that Sabbath, I took time to watch a few sessions beginning with Mike Bickle's message on "Abiding with the Lord." Such a tremendous focus on this: *"As the Father loved Me, I also have loved you; abide in my love."* (**John 15:9**). Oh, I loved this word. Then, *"…that the love with which you (the Father) loved me may be in thee."* These words are the very foundation of the Kingdom of God.

I was relishing every word. James was discussing with Mike the comments *first and great* regarding the commandments. *First,* people must grow in their love for God, and secondly, *excellent* refers to how we love God. Our love has the *most significant impact* on God's Heart and our hearts, and it is the *greatest calling.*

James was sharing how to prepare yourself as the Bride, and, to add humor, said, "Well, you could call Alexa to put on some Leslie Grant!" Well, my Amazon device, setting beside my computer, woke up! Wouldn't you know when he says have Alexa pull up some Leslie Grant, my machine came on, and Alexa announced the playlist of Leslie Grant.

Honestly, I didn't know of Leslie Grant, yet when I heard this music, I stopped everything. I got up and went to the living room listening to this lovely and touching words which caused me to realize my beautiful dancing days would be no more with Bob. He was asleep at the time—a tear formed as I got lost in her words and the loveliness of it all. I danced and pretended Bob was holding me.

You see, this had to be a God moment to help me remember all the dances we had. The Lord was calling me to never forget he has danced with me before, and he will dance with me again.

Remember, a gift from the Lord reminds you how treasured you are in His Heart.

"Every good and perfect gift is from above, coming down from the Father of the heavenly lights, who does not change like shifting shadows."
—*James 1:17 (NIV)*

SUNDAY MORNING PRAYER GROUP TEAR

MARCH 7TH

Sundays at 7a.m, I meet with two Godly gentlemen to pray, Pastor Stephen and Rolland. While we have specific things we are assigned to pray, it has also become a time to share precious things.

Rolland told us of how God had him at a stoplight, waiting for it to turn green. He became aware of a woman crossing the street coming from the direction of the Court House and heading to the bus station on the other side of the street. God had him there to witness a single tear falling down her right cheek. That God would highlight this touched his heart deeply. He went on to share he prayed every day for the woman with the tear.

That morning, when we were done with our prayers, I found myself thinking about this woman with the tear. I started praying for her too. Not much later, Bob, who was in the living room and yes, in his blue robe and fuzzy LLB slippers, called for me to come to him. For some reason, I knelt before him to really fix his gaze to discover a tear rolling down his right cheek. It was a breathless moment. I touched the tear and touched his mouth. The tear kept running, so I touched the tear to my mouth. Then I took his blue hanky and touched it again.

Suddenly, I knew God was showing me how much he loves Him. He was showing me he cares so deeply for us. This tear that touched our lips will remain with me as one of the most precious moments ever with my beloved partner. I knew at this moment never again to wonder about God's Presence. He just knows, so well, when to touch our hearts.

It takes our willingness to listen and wait for God to reveal Himself. Wait for the Lord to reveal Himself through our partners. Listen and let God speak first.

Remember a time when you listened with your heart. Were you able to handle the quiet moments? Learn to listen to God in the silence of your heart.

"Then you will call on me and come and pray to me, and I will listen to you."
—*Jeremiah 29:12 (NIV)*

SHIP AHOY

MARCH 8TH

Many years ago, my husband's father, who ran the Burpee Funeral Home in Rockland, ME, received as payment a lovely ship model to cover the cost for his wife's funeral. Measuring at least 38 inches long x 14 inches wide on the rigging, this three-masted beauty was the focal point over the fireplace for many years at Bob's home, the Roxmont Inn. It sat in front of a large and magnificent Maine Rocky Shore painting. The hearth was 10 feet wide. The size of this ship replica was perfectly suited to its stunning position.

Years later, Bob's father passed it along to Bob as the oldest child. John and Bill, Bob's sons, then young men, were on the Vineyard that summer. So off they went with the jeep up to Maine to pick it up. Alas, it came with its own special crate. With no place to put it, the hallway seemed best. The crate stayed there so long that I finally treated it as furniture. I placed a picture above it and probably something on top to make it look homey. This would have been in the '80s. Never, did it come out of the crate for the many years that followed.

In 2007 we sold the Vineyard home and took a leap of faith to move to Ft. Lauderdale, where we had been spending the winters aboard *Escapade,* our Hatteras Long Range Cruiser. Into storage, the beloved ship crate went along with everything else and didn't emerge until 2009 when we finally owned land and a home on the New River.

We took most of 2008 to remodel the entire home, including Bob's office with a custom section for this ship model. It finally had a perfect resting place. There it remained until we downsized to move to a condo in 2017; back into the crate it went to sit in the dark and wait for the next chapter.

Now, here we are in 2021 and ready to, once again, downsize. To whom will the ship go? Finally, on March 8th, in preparation for clearing our final large storage unit, I got on my knees and removed all the screws from one side of the crate. Oh, my goodness! There she was in perfect condition. It was a rather breathtaking moment to see her again! Finally, after much family deliberation, it was mutually decided to move this family treasure to sister Cyncy's oldest son Bob. As we speak, I am making the arrangements for it to hopefully have a final destination.

That afternoon, showing Bob pictures of his glorious ship once again, suddenly my husband became quiet and not feeling well. It seemed to pass quickly, yet a tear came down that right cheek again. I dried it and asked if he was okay. He quietly replied, "I guess I just didn't know how I would feel about this." This tear was about much more than a ship model.

We spoke, and again I knelt before him as before to let him know he had been a good steward and now another generation would take over. That tear came to me as a reminder that we are like this ship, waiting in the dark sometimes for God's Glory to appear to have our next steps revealed.

Remaining quietly inward with trust deepens our faith as we know the Lord will make all things work for the good of those who love Him. Our fruits will be known by our faithfulness. Every tear counts and collectively they all matter. Share your trust in the Lord to help someone in need. Help them shed their tears. Pray with them and for them.

What is your most recent time of tears? Did that moment enlarge your understanding to a higher perspective?

"God's glory is all around me! His wraparound presence is all I need, for the Lord is my Savior, my hero, and my life-giving strength. Trust only in God every moment! Tell him all your troubles and pour out your heart-longings to him. Believe me when I tell you he will help you."
—Psalm 62:7-8 (TPT)

"Be joyful in hope, patient in affliction, faithful in prayer. Share with the Lord's people who are in need. Practice hospitality."
—Romans 12:12 {NIV)

THE LITTLE RED GLOVES

MARCH 9TH

Today Bob had an appointment with the urologist. The office policy is that only the patient goes in, and they will call you if necessary to join them. There I was, sitting in the car using the newly acquired Handicap Parking Card. I had gotten "Red" out of the trunk and helped Bob through the office door. Then I waited for them to call me.

Thank goodness for "Red," which is a Drive Walker gift from our children for Christmas. I had parked it under the lovely Christmas tree in our condo foyer and led Bob downstairs to make the discovery! It was just the perfect gift to lift his spirits. "Red" has become his friend.

Moments later, they did call to come on in to meet the doctor. What I encountered was another God moment. There was a gentleman with the same Red Drive Walker. Quickly I could see his issue was not the walking so much but the breathing, as he had oxygen in his little zipper basket located on the front which holds essentials. His wife was so dear to him, adjusting his mask and making sure all was well. She patted his back. Soon they were asked to go on back to wait for the doctor. I couldn't help but notice as they passed before me the little pair of red leather boxing gloves attached to his handle.

I headed for Bob's room down the hall, and there we waited. He was seated in his "Red." Together we spoke sparingly. Soon a medical assistant took some notes; then the doctor himself appeared. He spoke gently in terms of having done all he could do. We spoke briefly about other appointments scheduled for Bob and to keep him informed. Then we waited for the assistant to come for his every-three month shot to control prostate cancer.

A comfortable silence was with us. I was thinking about what to say with this news, when Bob spoke and said softly, "Maybe I should just give up." "Quietly," I responded. "No Bob, the doctor is not saying to give up. He is saying what new areas we could explore." Yes, I had a tear. Then, I told him about the little red leather gloves on the other man's Red Drive. Those little boxing gloves equated to never giving up. We wouldn't either. No one was coming to give the shot, so more silence surrounded us. Suddenly, I began to regret using the Handicap Parking card. This couple needed that space way more than we did. I knew what we were going through and just paused to reflect. As I write this, I am blessing that couple with your Favor, Lord.

God shows us things to help us grow and find discernments on how we take in information. Those little red gloves will stick with me, as I discern how and why we never quit. Never. I ordered a pair of mini red leather gloves for Bob's Red.

Name a time you were tempted to give up but didn't. Did it deepen your resolve? Did you stand your ground?

"Blessed is the one who perseveres under trial because, having stood the test, that person will receive the crown of life that the Lord has promised to those who love him."
—*James 1:12 (NIV)*

WE HAD A BIT OF TROUBLE

MARCH 12TH

It was one of those mornings we needed to be up to leave for an appointment with Lauren. Lauren, our sound therapist who heals through sound frequencies, wanted us to come in early to have needed time to work with Bob.

I helped him get dressed and ready for breakfast. Checking the clock, all was on time and target for departure. I got myself ready and joined Bob for the remainder of his breakfast. We ate in silence. Sometimes the quiet seemed to speak louder than any words.

I brought out "Red" and helped him with his mask. We headed for the front door. He stepped out to the walkway and started for the elevator. I was only a moment behind Bob, checking one last time my purse for car keys before locking the door. After closing the door, I stepped onto the walkway. I could see him pushing his new Red Drive Walker into the fourth-floor elevator area. Oops, the Holy Spirit reminded me I needed to take his Xtandi medication to show Lauren. So, back I went quickly to retrieve it then walked briskly to the elevator foyer. Down I go to discover no Bob.

I asked Joe if he had seen Bob. No. I immediately went back to the fourth floor to search for him with no luck. I returned to the main floor. By now, Joe had called the maintenance guys whom I describe as angels! Armando and Ramon stopped what they were doing to help search for my missing man. Ramon went outside to see if he could see him pushing "Red" on some other floor. Armando headed to the second floor to check our old address. No Bob. He worked his way up to six then returned. Finally, Ramon said he would go to seven. Armando would go to the penthouse to make sure. Kim, another resident, went to the stairwells to search.

Alone, I refused to let the enemy begin to work on me with thoughts of him falling. Tears came. Not just one but many. I knelt by a chair and began to pray. I praised the Lord for showing us where he was. I spoke to the Lord, "Lord help us." Then, standing up, I began praising and thanking the Lord.

Ramon called to let me know he found him. I dried my tears. He was on seven, just sitting in his Red Drive machine, waiting. Bob was very calm and not one bit worried at all. The service elevator opened; out came Bob, still seated comfortably with Ramon pushing. Bob was unaware of the posse of people looking for him. He was in trust someone would show up. They all joked around with Bob as I silently thanked the Lord for revealing his location and blessing all who had pitched in to search. Armando helped me get him into the car, and off we went. I called ahead to Lauren we had a bit of trouble and would be late.

Lauren's meeting was so very fruitful. She helped us find the answer a battery of doctors was still seeking to consider. We left Lauren's feeling a new sense of relief from her uncovered revelations. Bob's trust in all the events touched me so much. We must go higher in our perspective to see more. That's what he did. We need to trust the Lord to show us our next steps. We need to pray over everything.

What I learned: Praise is my weapon. Praise and pray over every situation to call forth trust. Through praise God will deliver more than we ask. Through prayer we learn to prevail in God. This was a timely lesson of eliminating hurry to bring ease to all we do.

Remember a time you had trouble that kept you in worry in the night? Remember to praise and pray putting your trust in the Lord.

"Do not be anxious about anything but in every situation, by prayer and petition, with thanksgiving present your request to God."
—Philippians 4:6 (NIV)

DAY 7:
YOU ARE NOT ALONE

APRIL 6TH

It was Steven K's Sabbath Sermon of February 27th that turned the corner for my next steps. His message was to bring tears weeks later. Those powerful words on preparing the Bride, calling for rest to seek reflection, spoke to my soul. His Rest will always reveal the Lord's comforting love. His Love unveils the Joy and touches the heart with His Peace.

The last of his message spoke to my heart. The Lord's Love is a safe place. Never give up, and His Love is never defeated. I needed such a message as this, particularly today. I stayed online for personal prayers and was blessed to be alone with Brenda, a powerful Godly woman of prayer. She shared deeply with me the Lord's Word urging me to prepare to move my beloved to hospice. I found myself in denial as I assured her, he was not near the end. She stopped me to say, "Dianne, this is what the Lord is saying, not me."

I reflected on this that day with gratitude and put it aside for the moment. March came and went with stressful days of several falls in the night hours. The EMTs were so helpful and responded so very quickly. Those incidents began a series of signs that slowly, finally helped me rethink the denial in my heart.

The last week, as March's trials moved into April, I made the call. Nurse Carlie is my new friend. She came and spoke to us with tenderness about hospice. I waited for several days to talk it over with Bob before finally admitting him to their care here in our home. In obedience to the Lord. I found myself lifted to truly understand the care and comfort hospice offers so freely with their hearts of gold. Gold Coast Hospice is golden.

With nurses and aides in place and all other arrangements complete, I could place my full attention on what mattered most—my lifelong partner of 43 years. I wanted him to stay at home in our bed until his last breath was taken.

What have I learned? The Lord's Love transcends all things. He has given me a peace that only He can offer. The Holy Spirit now guided my days to keep me focused on Him and how I might touch the heart of my husband.

Come to Christ with your honesty. Feast on His Joy. Rekindle your altar fire for the Lord. He alone never changes. He is the same yesterday, today, and forever.

"Therefore, as God's chosen people, holy and dearly loved, clothe yourselves with compassion, kindness, humility, gentleness, and patience. Bear with each other and forgive one another if any of you has a grievance against someone. Forgive as the Lord forgave you."
—Colossians 3:12-13 (NIV)

"You are always and dearly loved by God! So, robe yourself with virtues of God since you have been divinely chosen to be holy. Be merciful as you endeavor to understand others, and be compassionate, showing kindness toward all. Be gentle and humble, unoffendable in your patience with others. V14 For love is supreme and must flow through each of these virtues. Love becomes the mark of true maturity. V15 Let your heart be always guided by the peace of the Anointed One, who called you to peace as part of his one body. And always be thankful."

—Colossians 3:12, 14-15 (TPT)

THOSE WHO SOW IN TEARS

APRIL 10TH

In the coming days, I discovered I could cry over most anything. Acts of kindness would be at the top of the list. What touched me most was the reaching out of the few close friends I had entrusted to know about the vigil I was keeping. I could not have learned on this day what or how events would unfold. It just seemed important to let close friends know. I didn't even know at this point my daughter, Abby, was about to appear. Jesus is so good watching over each of us.

What did happen this day? The entire hospice team assigned showed up all on the same day. Relief flooded my heart. The *Lord's Special Angelic Forces'* had arrived.

Thus, began the influx of support, angelic support. Each one was gracious in approaching Bob to become familiar with his conditions and demeanor. I knew this was a Godly and correct decision. Brenda was right to admonish me days before with, this is what the Lord says, *"Get Hospice."* Over the several days that followed, I pulled in my dear ones to walk with me embraced by their prayers.

Not in any special order, Mirelle, Tracey, Cathy, Mary, Nancy, Marilyn, Judy, Lori, Maureen, and Melanie, were some of the first to know.

Cousins Cathy and Mary began a series of brief, yet loving calls to see how we were doing. Upon hearing my news, Nancy sent gifts of food and flowers from Publix that same day. Judy nurtured me with special encouragements. Mirelle and Tracey, who both live in Australia, began a series of heart-warming letters. Jean K often called, as did Lisa P. Lisa D came with baby orchids. Melanie brought food and made herself available. Lori next door delivered banana bread. Mo brought us soup and a gorgeous white orchid. Oh, the outpouring. Neighbor Seena called and sent flowers, as did Sally and Glenna. Abby's colleague, Stephanie, sent a lovely planter. Even Kirk, the paperboy, dropped off a bouquet. Abby's friend Anna, living in Russia, sent a precious orchid arrangement. Betsy sent a book, *The Swallow, The Owl, and The Sandpiper* from the Sandpiper Trust. Cathy shared an encouraging book, *The Undistracted Widow*, by Carol W. Cornish. Marilyn's lilies kept on bringing me such peace. Maggie, from the Vineyard, and I had a long conversation supporting each other with our losses. Donna invited me to lunch, my first time out in weeks. My goodness, Lord, how you have blessed me. Sue was checking in. Corey extended thoughtful words. So many cards of comfort, Lord, and the love given from the Fort Lauderdale Woman's Club. You opened the Window of Heaven, Lord, to shower me with your comfort and peace.

Bob's dearest best friend, Jimmy Woods, called to arrange a visit. Coming from the west coast of Florida and being a military man, Woody arrived promptly at nine a.m. Bob was thrilled to see him. I left the two of them alone together. Gales of laughter made my heart sing. That would be Woody's style. Never a dull moment nor missed opportunity with his light-hearted sarcasm. He said goodbye to Bob. Woody and I knew it would be the last time to see him. We went to the balcony to take a few moments. I thanked him for coming and for being a faithful dear friend. It just touched me so much. A good friend moves heaven and earth when needed.

Bob's colleagues Ed, Fred, and Steve helped me have a fresh insight and greater perspective to understand the difference Bob had made with each of them in the marketplace. Bob was a mentor and a friend who was unquestionably successful. He helped them to achieve great levels of success with his training. He promised that never would they have a change of title; instead, the change would be in their financial reward by following his footsteps. I carried a new fresh understanding of Bob's clarity and focus. These guys opened my heart with these blessings.

That same day, Mirelle's email had a subject line, *"Thinking of you and sending love and blessings."* She reminded me those who *wait* upon the Lord renew their *strength*. The Hebrew word for wait encompasses being actively intertwined with the Lord and Lord intertwined with us in oneness, a unity of heart as we come and dwell in Him. She prayed for my being to be continually encouraged by the Holy Spirit *springs of living water* stored in my soul. Dearest friends really do matter.

These thoughts and prayers sustained the days that followed. Those living wells of water produced tears on demand. Only five days later, Abby arrived and took charge of the day-to-day needs allowing me to spend more time caring for Bob to just lay beside him. Eventually, I told a few more trusted friends, Jean, and my Faithful Four Prayer group. I had stopped attending other groups. I withdrew from outside news with no television nor taking phone calls. Yes, the news went off a few days before Abby arrived, and as of today's date, June 15th, a one-month milestone, I have yet to turn it back on. I stopped looking at emails on my computer at the end of March to remain quiet in waiting upon the Lord.

When you have trials to endure, it is wise to put aside all things for the Lord to direct your steps. Gather your valued friends to help you remain in the Lord's Presence and Power. It only takes one. You must say no to the many things robbing you of needed focus on the assignments the Lord gives you. Obedience requires intention backed by focus. In this way, you are creating a testimony for the Lord for His Strength to give you endurance coupled with faith to run the race.

"Those who sow in tears shall reap in joy. He who continually goes forth weeping, bearing seed for sowing, shall doubtless come again with rejoicing bringing his sheaves with him."
—Psalm 126:5-6 (NIV)

DAY 9:

NURSE HEIDI—ANGEL HEIDI

April 11th

Throughout the night, I was aware that Bob's breathing had changed. That morning I realized he had not changed positions. I listened for him and could hear nothing. Looking, I could see his chest still breathing. The events of the day before had taken him to a new level—weakness due to losing interest in food and little water. The sight of the sinking weight of his body was beyond what I could endure. A bathroom trip was going well until time to help him up. I cried out to the Lord for help. In gratitude, the Lord helped me get him to his bath chair. There we waited. His legs began to quiver. I held his head. He simply could not move. I called 911 for help.

The same EMTs, now familiar with our home and where to find us, rescued us. Little "Red" was used to move him closer to bed. Finally, he was safe again, laying down in exhaustion. He went into a deep rest.

This morning it hit me. Nurse Heidi came to bathe him, fully realizing a new level of release had occurred. She comforted me with her words, encouraging me to read *When Death is Near*. I had put it off and knew this was the day. Even then, I waited. Abby called, checking in around 2:30. By then, I lay beside him holding his hand, whispering the **23rd Psalm** and kissing his shoulder. He repeated, "The Lord restores my soul."

Dianne Congdon

The Lord had me move into talk of heaven and letting go. I knew the Divine Timing of the Lord was guiding me to help Bob finally give his heart to the Him. He repeated my words so sweetly. Tears of joy mixed with tears of loss. Yet, I know the Lord Jesus heard our soft whispers seeking confession, repentance, and forgiveness.

In the remaining hours and days, we reviewed the many memories we had created. We acknowledged together how we always left things better than when we found them. We reviewed the many ways we did this. You see, the Lord was with us during all our 43 years. We did have a Triune Blessing. That which was loosed on earth with Bob's giving of his heart to the Lord then became loosed in heaven.

What I learned about this day reassured me the Lord awaits each of us to repent and return to Him. He is so gracious with His Mercy allowing us time to transform our hearts by not walking with the world, only seeking His Kingdom to prepare ourselves as the Bride of Christ. His Love for us is unfailing.

Realize the Lord knows the end before the beginning begins. Place your life in His Hands to do as Bob has done; give your heart to Jesus. He tenderly will transform your life as you engage in Him. He is in you, and you are in Him. The Heavenly Father only fellowships with Himself. He fellowships with you, carrying the Father within you. The Father sent each of us the Holy Spirit to comfort and guide us. In this way, we can serve others.

"I will give you the keys to the kingdom of heaven, whatever you bind on earth will be bound in heaven, and whatever you lose on earth will be loosed in heaven."
—Matthew 16:19 (NIV)

On Love, *"It always protects, always trusts, always hopes, always perseveres. Love never fails."*
—1 Corinthians 13:7-8 (NIV)

ABBY TO THE RESCUE

APRIL 15TH

Why I thought I could do this by myself is beyond me. Now, as I look back to the arrival of beautiful Abby, the Lord was directing my steps with His Plan. She announced just days before she was coming and would not have it any other way. I protested not. It indeed was the Lord at work as we had not seen each other since pre-COVID, October 2019. At that time, she and brother Bill came on a rescue mission to clear out a storage unit. The days of 2020 drifted into prolonged isolation, so it was just thrilling to see her once again, finally. I could barely let her go at first.

She arrived at midnight the day before and after two nights at an Airbnb hotel then came to stay with us. We had determined the sofa bed would work for her in the office, which we now called the Vineyard Room. It displays our Vineyard treasures as well as Bob's beautiful desk and new office chair. He had used his new office chair only four times for eating breakfast. Abby works from home like most of America, so I quickly realized the office chair was never for Bob but her. God is so good.

Abby arrived at just the right moment. God's divine timing is always so perfect. The Lord is rarely early but never late. That day was the last time Bob was able to stand and walk. Her arrival helped me put into place a new level of care. With Abby there, I was now free to help Bob as needed. God is so good. Abby also stayed in communication with her brothers John, wife Sheila, and Bill, keeping them informed of Bob's condition as well as demeanor. She simply took charge of the details.

She quickly settled in her new room, setting up her workspace. By the next day, we had easily entered in a new rhythm. She, being the "Flower Queen". began shopping for food items and flowers. My goodness, she took our dining room table flowers to a new level! Every morning she trimmed stems and changed the water. It was her meditation ritual to care for flowers and plants first thing. It so lifted my spirit as well it was lovely to witness. Fresh flowers change the atmosphere. Abby changes the atmosphere wherever she goes.

The day after she arrived, I had scheduled my first outside appointments, which I had not been able to do. Abby later told me she sat with Bob the entire time, talking about his childhood and early years. The conversation turned to the long-held *Hubbard Platter*. It had been given to Bob by his mother sometime in the '60s. It lived in the Vineyard house, obscure and hidden in a chest. Little did we know what enormous value it held until the Lord guided Abby to go to Ancestry.com to look at his family history.

Robert Milton Leach, Bob's namesake and grandfather's lineage, was from the Hubbard Family who migrated to America for religious freedom. Blessed by the Lord, this family has grown into thousands who primarily live on America's soil and all over the world. Bob's family migrated from Ipswich, England, aboard vessel *Defense* in 1635 and helped establish Ipswich, Massachusetts. William Hubbard and wife Judith Knapp, 1635, was the first listed on the chronological order of the Hubbard family line on a plaque attached to the platter. His grandfather, Robert Milton Leach, is the last listing dated 1921. Bob's mother, Virginia Leach, 2001, would be listed as the 10th and Bob 11th.

Abby ordered that same day a book entitled, *1000 Years of Hubbard History*. There began the nightly readings about Bob's generational line. It turned out Bob knew all about Hubba, along with Hinga, who officially started the Hubbard Family Name around AD 867 after capturing land which eventually became Ipswich, England. Who knew? It caused me to realize how humble Bob was. It caused me to reflect on humility and walking without pride. Abby opened a door we didn't know existed. I brought home the mysterious Hubbard Platter, which was once regarded as *that old thing*), from obscurity in our storage unit to a place of honor on our bookcase seat. We both agree this platter belongs in a museum. We vowed to explore this.

Abby's arrival not only lifted my spirits, but it also touched Bob's heart deeply that she was here. It was such a great lesson to allow someone to help us. She helped so much with Bill and John, to be included often by phone with their father. She made such a difference. It made me realize I was working out of pride in my ability to do it all. Well, her arrival brought several gifts, physically and spiritually.

Is there any area where you are isolating yourself from those who want to help? It reminded me, the Lord wastes nothing and brings all things together for your good.

"And we know that in all things God works for the good of those who love him, who have been called according to his purpose."
—Romans 8:28 (NIV)

AN ANOINTED DAY

APRIL 26TH

We were entering our 3rd week with Gold Coast Hospice, otherwise known as the Gold Coast "Angels." Aide Heidi had not yet come for bathing when Chaplain Ken showed up. Bob welcomed him, and together we all took a moment to praise the Lord for this very day. The **23rd Psalm** came to my mind, so I went to the kitchen to get the anointing oils. We three, Ken, Bob, and I, held hands and spoke the **23rd Psalm**.

When it came to **Verse 9**: *You anoint my head with oil*, I handed Ken the Frankincense that dries white so dying to oneself and doing the Will of the Father, followed by the Calamus Root Oil for strength of a holy character. Then, Cinnamon Oil is walking upright in the righteousness of the Lord and, finally, Esther's Oil of Myrrh for turning the bitterness to an Oil of Joy. Ken applied them reverently on Bob's forehead, all of which genuinely anointed not only Bob but each of us with His Presence. God had Ken show up at just the right time. God provides the unexpected blessings when we put Him First. We thanked Ken for his prayers.

It seemed like the right time as well to visit the need for forgiveness. Bob's heart was touched and had opened to receive the anointing blessing. Now was the time to deal with specific family issues that had been on my mind. The Holy Spirit had long been planting this subject in my soul. We discussed the wounds he had been carrying from witnessing divorce between his mother and father at ages 5-6. We searched even more for the need to seek forgiveness and to offer forgiveness. Bob agreed, and so carefully I suggested writing a letter to both his father and mother to seek healing. We also had many calls from his boys, Bill, and John, with wife Sheila. It was important; while they weren't with the daily care, they were needed to play an active role in healing with offering their love and emotional support. Bob did his best to bless them.

Then, his brothers and sisters came up next. Again, with caution, I asked if I could write them a letter seeking forgiveness and healing. He said yes. It took several days before the right words appeared and suddenly flowed from my pen. I wrote identical letters to his brother and sister. I read them to his sister Cyncy, who had been close to him all these years. She, too, felt it a very positive act of kindness. Then, I shared with Bob who seemed pleased with my message, so off they went in the mail. I then realized Bob was letting go of all that had deeply hurt him. The Lord Jesus takes care of forgiveness when we turn to Him. I still cry every time I recall this day. Bob was preparing to leave in his own way.

Embracing Bob with love and nurturing was bringing us closer to the Lord. It became my assignment that called for obedience and strength. It was helping birth him spiritually into his glorious Eternal Life. What I learned was with all things we do, there are two sides to consider: the actions taken at the natural level will always be equipped in the spiritual from the Lord. In every step, we assume there are Holy Spirit Impartations to bless us when we awaken to it. All forgiveness begins in the heart.

Think for a moment of some ordinary things you do that could take on a new and deeper meaning by seeking the Holy Spirit's blessing for added wisdom and revelation to offer forgiveness.

"I can do all things [which He has called me to do] through Him who strengthens and empowers me [to fulfill His purpose—I am self-sufficient in Christ's sufficiency; I am ready for anything and equal to anything through Him who infuses me with inner strength and confident peace.]"
—Philippians 4:13 (AMP)

"Bear with each other and forgive one another if any of you has a grievance against someone. Forgive as the Lord forgave you."
—Colossians 3:13 (NIV)

A DAY OF HEALING

May 5th

Bob and I spent many hours that day reflecting on our years together. Snuggled together in bed, we recalled how we met and learned to know each other. We began to review our life together, all the places we visited, and the homes where we made our havens together. Our rule was always to leave a place better than we found it. We reflected on our life at Martha's Vineyard with all the lobsters, fishing, beaches, and boating. We reveled in watching the sun setting over water in the late afternoons. Forty-three years later, it was time to move on. We revisited the great Garage Sale Day. It was time to leave the Vineyard behind.

Abby was with us when we had a huge garage sale. We planned this several weeks before the mover was to come. Abs staged it in every room of our downstairs. Clothes, kitchen, dishes, books, fishing stuff, and on and on. A professional photographer friend loaned her his camera to capture all these special moments, including an art sale the following weekend from the barn studio where I had painted many summers. She added all the unique places on the Vineyard as well as our gardens and home. Bob had built this home with his first wife, Patricia Wilson Congdon, in 1965. Most importantly, it offered the magnificent views of the ocean and bays that surrounded the island and Menemsha Harbor, where we kept our boat. His family thought Bob to be crazy to buy land and build a home in such a remote place. Little did they know the sea brought him there and would be a central thread in the tapestry of his life.

Bob grew up loving the sea. His father Stafford, and mother, Virginia Leach Congdon, had purchased a beautiful home called Roxmont in Rockport, Me, close to Rockland where he was born. As a little boy, Bob could see the West Penobscot Bay from his bedroom window. Then, his grandfather, Robert Milton Leach, his namesake, taught him boating skills in a wooden craft on Webster Lake in Franklin, NH. Later, as a teen, he was crew on a sailing vessel. He loved the wind and the waves. I tell you this so that you could have a sense of Bob's peace he desired and had found on the Vineyard.

Back to my original letters asking for forgiveness of last week. There we were, snuggled in bed together, talking and reflecting on our life that morning. I remembered Abby's lovely photo "journey" she had created for our final departure from the Vineyard established throughout those Vineyard years. So, I asked Bob, "Should I get the book and let us relive it?" Quietly and after a while, he said, "No, I couldn't bear it."

That day was profound because his answer told me he had come to grips with dying. He would do it his way. The Lord was calling him Home. Such a blessing when letters arrived from both his sister, Diana, and brother, Malcom the same day. Pat Congdon, his first wife and mother of their boys, had written as well. They were beautiful confirmations of forgiveness and filled with recollections of their early childhood. I suggested we call his sisters and brother to acknowledge them and tell them how much we love them. We called them, as well as John, Sheila, and Bill to make, which I realized at the time was a loving final goodbye.

God showed me that day it is never too late to seek forgiveness. I learned the Lord, who does the forgiving, is present in every situation. Joy comes from knowing the Lord God never leaves us. His Holy Spirit *empowers* and *guides* us. The precious Lord moves us to the promise of eternal life when we believe and trust in Him.

Every time you thank the Heavenly Father in silent prayers, songs of praise, or time spent in reflection, you increase your joy which lifts you above every circumstance.

"So then, just as you received Christ Jesus as Lord, continue to live your lives in Him, rooted and built up in Him, strengthened in the faith as you were taught, and overflowing with thankfulness."
—*Colossians 2:6-7 (NIV)*

THE FEATHER

MAY 8TH

The days went by. Abby continued to take the heavy load of shopping and meals. Around her work schedule and various appointments, she graciously helped me with Bob. Every day had its rhythm. Early mornings she went to the Everglades House pool to swim before heading to the office. One afternoon, she decided to go for a walk to refresh herself after a taxing morning of meetings.

Little did I know she had picked up a feather. She happened to look down, she told me, to see it before her on the path. *Pick me up.* I knew nothing of it until the following day when I came out from the bedroom over to the table of Abby's freshly cut flowers. She comes alive with flowers as I mentioned earlier.

Abby's great love is arranging flowers. She has taken classes on flower arranging as well as how to care for them. She searches for just the right buds and colors. The first thing she did after arriving on April 15th was go to Whole Foods and buy flowers. She taught me to trim stems daily with a fresh uptake of water filled to the top of the vase. Uncut stems shorten their life. She brought home two gorgeous hydrangeas and placed them in my tall black pottery vase with an exotic palm leaf. The secret to a long-lasting hydrangea is to cut the stems back on an angle, then place them in a vase filled to the top with hot water. They lasted two weeks as a testimony to her method! Cut the stem on a slope, fill every vase up to the top daily, and add hot water when arranging hydrangeas, were Abby's flower tips!

So, I approached the table of cut and freshened flowers to find this feather right on the edge. It sat there all alone, which caught my eye immediately. I called Abby to come to look, asking her did this come from her? In astonishment, "Yes, Mother, but I placed it in your keyring last night." The Lord was leaving us a love note. Find peace and contentment in Him.

This feather will be with me for the rest of my life. When you walk with the Lord, you are never alone. He will hand-tailor a sign just for you. These gifts arrive daily. Seek them, and you will find your joy restored.

"But godliness with contentment is great gain. For we brought nothing into the world, and we can take nothing out of it."
—1 Timothy 6: 6-8 (NIV)

A BIRTHDAY TO CHERISH

MAY 12TH

Abby's birthday dawned on a beautiful Florida sunshine day! Bob and I had practiced singing "Happy Birthday" several days before. That day, however, he spoke little and seemed so distant. I had already gathered our gifts for her and prepared our cards along with a cake. Birthdays come and go. This one, however, for Abby will give reflection.

Thinking about how her birthday was made me realize it is not about what but who. Who you are and whose you are. It is about feeling cherished. That took me back in reflection to our second May birthday in the family—Bob's on May 26th.

On May 26, 2017, Bob turned 80. I arranged for us to fly to Boston to visit with Abby, Eric, and Amelia. We stayed in a nearby hotel and took them all to dinner. We so enjoyed visiting with them and seeing their charming place. It is a two-story home in Medford, MA. They occupy the second floor. Eric, who plays piano and practically every instrument known, arranged at their moving in time to have a crane to help bring his grand piano through a set of second-floor windows. I could not imagine it.

They loved the area and especially this place because of the high ceilings, offering a great sound and presence for the baby grand's new home. As Abby would say, music is our jam. During the COVID months, Eric composed and posted his newest compositions with a visual image nearly daily. Just so amazing. God brought these two together through music. He plays, and she sings. Abby also plays guitar and formerly played in a band called The NAB Band. Eric's has three other partners in a group called The Eric Ostling Quartet. Seeing them was such a delight. We just loved seeing them in their surroundings!

The following day we drove north in our rental car and headed to Maine, going through Freeport, ME, home of LLBean, which Bob always referred to as his haberdasher! After a few purchases, we headed on up to the rocky coast of Rockland, ME, where Bob was born. The kids planned a few surprises for his 80th Birthday. A day trip with a lobster fisherman was one of them.

Out we go with another passenger to learn all about lobstering. Going from pot to pot was such fun on that beautiful spring May Day. It was the day before the actual birthday. We learned all about baiting the car, pulling the wire crate, and banding the lobbies. We took it all in as if we knew nothing. What Bob didn't tell them was we had a family lobster license on the Vineyard. Bob had 10 pots, and we had lobster for Sunday dinner. It had been nine years or more since those days. Still, we just loved it so much because it was just off the lighthouse point of Rockland. We had dinner at our favorite restaurant, Primo's, to finish off the perfect celebration. It is all about what you cherish and who you cherish.

Birthdays shouldn't count, and they don't belong in heaven. Age is about attitude! You are as young as you think, not what the calendar says. It is just so unique, though, when something remarkable occurs to lock in that memory, like a birthday spent in Maine.

Abby's birthday dinner was like all other nights in our bedroom so we could be with Bob in hopes he would take in a bite. That night he seemed very quiet. The next day, however, Abby and I will always feel it being a precious moment when Bob helped me sing "Happy Birthday" to her. Barely, with a whisper, he got through the first two Happy Birthdays and fell silent. Now, that is a birthday gift to treasure.

Cherish each moment because it is a blessing from God. They become the memories you store in your heart spaces that later bless and refresh your soul.

"I have loved you with an everlasting love; I have drawn you with unfailing kindness."
—Jeremiah 31:3 (NIV)

THE LORD'S CALLING

MAY 14TH

Recalling this was Friday, I awakened early as usual and tended to Bob's needs. By then, I was lost in time, now thinking that this day would be four weeks of him being in bed. Just days before, in some of his last conversation, he asked, *"Am I ever going to get out of here?"* Yes, my darling, and it will be soon.

Heidi, the nurse's aide, wanted me to know she was going out of town the next day for a week; could she come for Bob's bath. Her husband surprised her with a trip to unknown places. We were happy for her! After she was done, she told Bob goodbye and would see him in a week. He replied, *"If I am still here."* Heidi and I looked at each other.

Weeks before, Sonja, an RN, had given me the book, *When Death is Near*, which I have mentioned before. Remember how I couldn't bear to read the last pages listing the things to look for? Well, I got the book out again for Abby and me to reread. The Holy Spirit was now guiding us to be alert to the signs. As painful as this was, I found myself throughout the day being so watchful. Bob was in another place with no more words.

The day went on as I lay with him, whispering love notes to him. We had said the **23rd Psalm** often together these past weeks. He always stopped after, *"He leads me beside the still waters where he restores my soul."* I could hardly bear it.

Night came; the day was done. I found myself unable to do the usual getting ready for bed. I put on my workout clothes and got back in bed with him. Labored breathing continued, so I shifted him to his side to help. He quieted some. At 11:30 or so, I called for Abby to come.

What happened next will remain beautiful moments only Abby and I will know. I will tell you we stayed up all night to review and help each other realize our assignment was over. I did not think I could cry another tear, yet they just didn't stop. After sunrise, we called the boys and Bob's sisters and brother to let them know. Bob would not reach his 85th birthday on May 26th.

The Love of my life was Called Home by the Lord.

Do not wait to show love to your beloveds. Honor what they ask you for as it will become your memories. Do not wait to offer forgiveness to those in your life. You know who they are. Be honest with yourself about your life. The Lord must come first. Your weakness will lead you to the Lord, who will provide you strength in your time of need.

"The Lord will work out his plans for my life—for your faithful Love, o Lord, endures forever... "
—Psalm 138: 8 (NIV)

NO NEED TO EMAIL—JUST REST

MAY 25TH

With Abby leaving in a couple of days, we decided to quietly celebrate Bob's birthday. We were busy wrapping up several details and beginning to plan Bob's Celebration of Life. It was then I realized I was about to be alone to face my next steps. Bravely, I told myself, if my mother could do this, then I can do this. I remember pausing to recall her strength, courage, and never complaining about a thing.

Two days later, the reality was to set in. It was the weekend which turned into a bit of a blur. Good grief, I would have to do my own food shopping again, so that became my first step back out in some sort of rhythm.

By then, as I let people know about Bob being Called Home, many cards began to arrive. I had gathered my cards, pens, and envelopes to write each one how much I appreciated their caring words. Abby designed a lovely tribute card for Bob which turned out to touch many hearts. I used it to thank our friends for caring. As well, I decided it was time over to tackle the emails. I discovered 5400+ of them and immediately began the deleting process. It took me three days to delete them, saving 197 ones of importance. Among the emails were caring words from Mirelle.

Mirelle's subject line: Comfort and Love. "Resting in the Lord will be beautiful— and I pray for protection by the Precious Blood to keep you and shield you with Jesus' seal upon you—in the time—this season— this area. So glad your neighbors are lovely as this is a great blessing, Dearest Dianne."

In the days that followed, she blessed me with this worship song and poetry.

MY LIFE IS BUT A WEAVING

"My life is but a weaving
Between my God and me.
I cannot choose the colors
He worketh steadily.
Sometimes He weaveth sorrow
And I in foolish pride
Forget He sees the upper,
And I the underside.

Not till the loom is silent
And the shuttles cease to fly,
Shall God unroll the canvas
And explain the reasons why.
The dark threads are as needful
In the Weaver's skillful hand
As the threads of gold and silver
In the pattern, He has planned.

My life is but a weaving
Between my God and me;

I see the seams, the tangles,
But He sees perfectly,
He knows He loves, He cares,
Nothing this truth can dim
He gives His very best to those
Who chose to walk with Him.
Who leave the choice to Him."

CHO-WA

MAY 27TH

Abby was with me seven weeks by my side. Now, she needed to return to life in Boston. I could hardly bear to see her go. After dropping her off, I returned to the quiet of our place. I guess now it was my place. We had a beautiful day of wrapping up the last details and committed to making plans.

One of the things we discussed was my attending, in July, the 100th Centennial High School Reunion in my hometown of Holyrood, Kansas. Together, we decided it was a good thing as my brother would be attending. In addition to seeing classmates, it would be the first time in over 10 years to see him. Abby helped me find the best fares. We sealed the deal with dates, rental cars, and calls, to arrange for overnights on both ends with family and friends.

The day was quiet and reflective as I prepared for bed. My first night alone was more sleepless than anything. It was not at all being afraid but more dealing with my deep sadness. Dealing with the many years and plans we had put off, especially to return to visit Maine and his birthplace. In coping with this precious loss, my bed felt so empty. I hugged his pillow.

Friday, the next morning, I had already planned to begin a new thing when this first new day alone arrived. Years ago, I received a booklet in the mail simply entitled Cho-Wa. It intrigued me, so after reading, I was hooked and ordered this ancient Japanese Tea. The booklet contains the remarkable story of Japan's legendary healing formula and how it continues to work wonders.

Several weeks before, I once again discovered this book. So, that morning I decided to reread the book. In it was a note from the desk of Dr. Hiro Kumato dated June 9, 2011. "Dear Bob, this book will change your life. Enjoy! HK." Tears upon tears came. I put the "what ifs" aside as I was determined to have no regrets about the many months of trials we had gone through, ending in four weeks of being in bed with Hospice Home Comfort Care. I was determined to turn my trials to testimonies for the Lord.

I decided to order it once again. When it arrived, I chose a special blue cup for the Cho-Wa and put a packet on top, awaiting the first day I would be alone. It sat on the countertop amid all my blue kitchen pottery. After waking that morning, I did my singing the **23rd Psalm** to the Lord with anointing oils and my daily communion with Him.

My heart knew to honor my first full day alone with Cho-Wa. I decided in anticipation, from this day forward, the Lord directs my steps for His Plans and Purposes. I fully submitted my heart to Him. He became my husband. I opened my chronological Bible to May 27th and began reading from **Proverbs 3:1-35** on Lessons for Daily Life. I especially was touched by **V1** "My child, never forget the things I have taught you. Store my commands in your heart. If do this, you will live many years, and your life will be satisfying," **V3** "Never let loyalty and kindness leave you! Tie them around your neck as a reminder," and **V5** "Trust in the Lord with all your heart; do not depend on your own understanding." It spoke to me so strongly that I decided to read my Bible first before all things every morning, not before going to bed as I had been doing. I was ready to make the Word my priority along with the **23rd Psalm** and Daily Communion, my protection with the Blood of the Lamb. I also committed to not only read the Word beginning with **Genesis** but also to study the Word to receive a deeper wisdom from the Lord.

Reading my Bible first thing while sipping my first cup of Cho-Wa in many years lifted my spirits. The Holy Spirit was at work to let me know you can do this. You will get through this. You are mine, and you will always be protected.

My first day alone reset my commitment to consecrate myself to serving the Lord for His Purpose and His Plan for me.

The Lord is calling you to seek His Plans and Purpose for you. Be intentional about this with Sacred Times with the Lord. Sit with Him in the quiet of your altar. Speak to Him, and He will come to you. Listen with your heart to know your next steps.

"Don't be pulled in different directions or worried about a thing. Be saturated in prayer throughout each day, offering your faith-filled requests before God with overflowing gratitude."
—Philippians 4:6 (TPT)

"For your Maker is your husband—the Lord Almighty is his name The Holy One of Israel is your Redeemer; he is called the God of all the earth."
—Isaiah 54:5 (NIV)

DAY 18:
MY BOO

MAY 28TH

This was to be my first day alone. I began this day, as you read earlier, with my return to Cho-Wa. Part of the joy comes from the ritual of slowly adding the hot water and stirring with intention. I love watching how it circles then rests in a pattern. This act alone brings me peace. God is all about order, patterns, and peace.

This was the appointed day I was to pick up Bob's ashes. I decided not to write about this the day before, the 27th, because I just couldn't. Now, with time I can share. Learning the cremation was underway, I was told the ashes would be ready to pick up the next day. This was nearly unbearable. To think of him without his body was difficult. Yes, I know the spirit and soul have departed, yet coming to grips with it is another thing. My tears turned to howls of grief at certain moments. The Holy Spirit was guiding me every step of the way.

I prepared my cup of Cho-Wa and gave thoughts to my day. I carefully dressed, which I do every morning as I prepare myself for any day. I think it stems from my mother giving me a box of her dresses, high heels, gloves, hats, and pearls, to play dress up as a little 6 or 7-year-old girl. I can still see myself acting all grown up in heels too big for my little feet trapping around the grass playing dress-up. I am still playing dress-up as a grown woman. It is a part of who I am. So yes, I dressed in care that morning to pick up my lover and dearest friend.

Leroy met me at the funeral home. He assisted Abby with listing Bob's Obituary as well as helped me that morning. Barbara Falowski had established this funeral service many years ago and personally served Broward General's Gold Coast Hospice herself. She was intimately involved. When I inquired about which funeral home to use, of course, it would be this one. My subsequent most beautiful discovery was to remember the current owner was a dear friend, Liz Frenier. I met her through the Ft. Lauderdale Woman's Club. She was instrumental in helping me get through all this. Wonderful people.

Leroy answered the door and helped me finalize the paperwork necessary for Bob to come home with me. I thanked him profusely for all the grace given throughout these days. How beautiful it is to do the work of the Lord, helping others with grief and loss. Heaven's gain through such a place as this. Leroy asked if I needed help in carrying Bob's urn to the car. I tested it and said, "No, I can do this."

Here's where "My Boo" comes in. Bob and I had discussed the need to get a new car. Our Ford Fusion was now eleven years old and often needing significant repairs. Maybe you have been in such a place with cars. I loved my car. I loved the custom leopard mats and "Fordy's" sage green color. Bob's 6'4" frame, however, struggled with getting in and out, especially when not feeling so great. Shopping for a new replacement was impossible, so we just continued to agree yes, we needed a new car. I always said a new, used car. Well, *pre-owned* is how they say it.

Abby came, and like a house of fire, she took charge at some point past midway of her seven weeks with me to address the need for a new car.

To this day, every single person remarked on this most beautiful gift of time she offered me. She took it upon herself to go the Ford dealer and test drive all that looked possible. We are talking *used* here, my friends, not new. Not feeling wildly inspired, she went across the street and down south to the Bayview Cadillac dealer. It was there she spotted "Boo", an XT4 in a mystery color called Shadow Metallic. It wasn't grey, and it wasn't blue.

So, not long after Bob's passing, Abby wanted to make sure she helped me with a new vehicle before returning to Boston. She made an appointment with Daniel. "Be careful because his eyes are gorgeous, Mother, and he will dazzle you." Oh, how right she was. Daniel was with another client, so his associate, Mark, took us on a test of the XT 4 and 5. Clearly, just seeing them both together, I fell in love with the "4." Nervously, Mark instructed me where to go to test each of them. The Holy Spirit quickly guided me) to the "4", for sure. I just knew what I needed to know.

Picture four salesmen, including "dazzling-eyes" Daniel standing there with, *"Well, ladies, are you ready to buy?"* I smiled and said, "We will think about it, and thank you so very much." Out to the car we go. Abby turned on "Fordy," then paused. She turned to me and said, "Shall I go back in there?" "Yes," I said. She turned off the car and headed back to begin the process. So, I stayed in the car for the next hour, waiting. I knew it was a done deal. Abby's brother, John from Scottsdale, was on the phone with her in negotiations helping to "seal the deal." Success! Congratulations were in order! Oh Lord, this was just so amazing! Then on to the financing department and our extraordinary meeting of Terak. That could be another story, I am thinking. We loved this guy.

What was remarkable, was that after four hours to complete the process, they kept "Fordy" and gave me the keys to drive the new car home without even owning it yet. We rejoiced at how the Lord had led us through this day. I prayed Bob would approve. He was always for American-built cars. Abby and I felt sure he would support our decision. We were thrilled beyond! We returned the next day in the afternoon to finish the paperwork.

So, as I walked across the funeral home parking lot, I introduced Bob to our new car. I strapped him in the front seat and headed for home. We talked along the way. Well, I did all the talking about how the Holy Spirit led us to this fantastic acquisition. "My Boo Caddy" was feeling happy too. We all were.

Before Abby left, we installed OnStar, which called for an account name. Abs had often called me "Boo." Out of the blue, I chose "My Boo Caddy". This service which offers so much support, gave me peace of mind and protection in driving a used car but was new to me. I gave my deepest gratitude to the Lord as He guided us through this entire process. When we seek Him and seek Him with all our heart, His Presence attends us. He was present. "Thank you, Jesus."

Trust the Lord with all your heart to allow the Holy Spirit to guide you and give you comfort. Trust only in God every moment! Tell Him all your troubles and pour out your heart to Him. Believe me when I tell you…He will help you. Placing your trust gives you protection as He guides with His Peace flooding your being. Seek Him always. You are His Bride. He loves you more in a moment than anyone could love you in a lifetime.

"If the Spirit is the source of our life, we must also allow the Spirit to direct every aspect of our lives."
—Galatians 6:25 (TPT)

"Give God the right to direct your life, and as you trust him along the way, you'll find he pulled it off perfectly!"
—Psalm 37:5 (TPT)

What seems impossible to endure becomes possible with the Lord.

Few words will matter during such a time as this. It's the Lord's Presence that heals.

"Jesus looked at them and said, 'With man this is impossible, but with God all things are possible.'"
—Matthew 6:26 (NIV)

ALONE AGAIN NATURALLY

JUNE 7TH

Music changed the atmosphere in the days before Bob's going to the Light. He loved Neil Diamond! We had gone to one of his concerts and would turn up the volume whenever we played Neil's songs! We started the morning with meditation music followed by Earl Klugh around 2 p.m. By 5, we would put on Neil! *Welcome to America!* Bob would tap his foot and smile. Diana Krawl's in her song, *Alone Again Naturally*, always brought me to tears. Abby would turn her off. I continued to play soaking music every day since replacing all news. Months have gone by now and still no news. Soft music, however, brings has brought me a sense of peace.

God knows naturally all we need and when we need it. As followers, we are surrounded by Him, filled with the Holy Spirit. Imagine God's Holy Spirit is always with you, guiding, bringing comfort, and leading you in the way to go. My body rushes when the Holy Spirit confirms. When we walk by faith, the Holy Spirit becomes our confidence in what we hope for and assurance about what we do not see. Without faith it is impossible to please God. God had long ago put together prayer partners who would support my faith. Among them, the Eagles.

The Convocation Eagles acquired this new name when our beloved and only male partner, David Finley, moved away due to demands from homeschooling his children. The formerly 7 Oaks were now Eagles: June, Sandy, Sandra, Donna, Marie and me. On this day, the Eagles Soared.

God knit us together for a purpose. Isn't that how everything happens, though? It is always for His Glory and Purpose. Marie and I had taken the *I Was Busy Now I'm Not* class back in 2018 and were asked to be small group coaches for the new class that had formed in 2019. It started out with 18 lovely souls from all over the world, not just America, and ended up with seven in our small group by the end of the course, then six without David. Empower 2000, the largest provider of Kingdom Based Webinars, used the small group concept to give each person a voice with intimacy, trust, and to deepen faith.

These prayer partners prayed for me through my final four weeks with Bob. Once Abby had returned to Boston, I needed to embrace *being alone*. The first days were so tender I could hardly speak of it. I needed the quiet to relish all the feelings and emotions that were coming. I honored every single tear. I considered every good and bad memory to help me forgive, heal, and let go. I was told and feel it true it takes about six weeks to fully allow the Lord to take you through the days of grieving after your beloveds have passed. Of course, but not always as it may take far longer as each situation is unique to the Lord.

June 7th was planned to resume the Eagles' monthly meeting, usually on a Monday. The day before, I began to shift my focus to the joys of remembering our journey. At the 23rd day mark after Bob's passing, my reflection just naturally flowed as I prepared for our gathering. After missing both April and May, we had much to cover. However, the attention turned to me. They wanted to hear my story. For my part, I had pulled together a few points to share. It turned out to be one of the most intimate and healing exchanges only the Holy Spirit could arrange.

I began with **Ecclesiastes 7:3**, "Sorrow is better than laughter, for sadness has a *refining influence* on us." That transformed and allowed me to stay in the moments to take all the sweetness I could possibly feel. Staying quiet was my answer. Saying no was the secret. *Focus on what you have*, not what you don't have.

I shared while I no longer had Bob's physical presence, yet I felt it such an honor to be entrusted in *helping birth* him to the Lord's Eternal Life. I shut out the world, its news, and chaos, to keep my heart clear about my mission, my assignment. Finally, I spoke of *accepting each day* God gives us and see the joys in them. I told the Eagles I felt I had stepped into a *"River of Light"* during those days. This day the Eagles soared into a new level of intimacy with the Holy Spirit guiding.

Every day counts because you never know the timeline of the Lord. Live in intention, knowing that what you say and do or do not do will change the atmosphere wherever you go. Be on assignment with the Lord as His Ambassador.

It is my prayer this novella which is based not on fiction, rather my testimony, will bring you or someone in your life, to love the Presence of the Holy Spirit. Invite His Power to transform your life through a renewal of your mind. Be intentional with your life. Do not care what others think, say, or do. It is none of your business. Walk in the confidence of the unseen. Love the Lord with all your heart. Do it now. Love His Word for therein lies your life's meaning.

"So be very careful how you live, not being like those with no understanding, but live honorably with true wisdom, for we are living in evil times. Take full advantage of every day as you spend your life for his purposes."
—Ephesians 5:15-16 (TPT)

"And out of your reverence for Christ, be supportive of each other in love. For wives, this means being devoted to your husbands like you are tenderly devoted to the Lord."
—Ephesians 5:21 (TPT)

"... but those who hope in the Lord will renew their strength. They will soar on wings like eagles; they will run and not grow weary; they will walk and not be faint."
—Isaiah 40:31 (NIV)

FLOUR AND OIL

JUNE 10TH

So, why *"Flour and Oil"* you ask. Just read **1 Kings 17:14**, "Elijah and the Widow" story where she trusted the Lord to use her *last flour and oil* to make bread for Elijah. He assured her she would never run out of flour or oil until the day the Lord sends rain on the land. Elijah brought her son back to life through the Lord. Imagine the security of seeing your flour jar always full. Your oil never running low. This is what the Lord can do for you.

The Lord is sending you this message of the "Flour and Oil" day to trust Him in all things. He will multiple your needs through your obedience. My "Flour and Oil" showed up on this day.

I just hadn't gotten my head around being a widow. Being alone brought me a new understanding of never being alone with the Lord. I sought the Father God as *Yahweh, God as my Husband* for counsel on many things in these past days just as I would have with Bob. Talking over circumstances for guidance.

It came through prayer partners Stephen Guarneros and Rolland Abraham. In February, Stephen called to see if I would join Rolland and his weekly prayer meetings, creating a three-strand cord. This was the

Lord's preparing for me the support that would be needed later. I could not possibly know this or imagine two months later Bob would be Called Home. God knew and sent me "Flour and Oil" ahead which will never run out. They became my flour and oil. Their prayers sustained me so profoundly through these days. I told them, **V24** *"Now I know that you are men of God and that the word of the Lord from your mouth is the truth."*

We must awaken now to being Called to our Kingdom Purpose in the Great Harvest of Souls. Every single person reading this is called to a destiny and purpose placed on their life in the Body of Christ. Each of us must focus on how we are to be a laborer in the field for the Lord. Look around you to see everything is being *shaken*. Step into this River of Light, and you will be shown your next steps. You will be given your Flour and Oil.

Do not go this alone. Seek the Lord for your comfort and healing. He will show you precisely how to move forward when you consecrate and submit to Him. Mary poured her costly Spikenard Oil over His head to anoint Jesus and prepare Him for burial. She washed His feet with her tears. Then she broke the costly alabaster jar. Seek your personal breakthrough into a new level of trust and faith with the Lord Jesus Christ. He is waiting for you to sit at His Feet.

"The Lord heals the brokenhearted and binds up their wounds."
—Psalm 149:3 (NIV)

"The Lord is near to all who call on him."
—Psalm 145:18 (NIV)

IN REMEMBRANCE

ROBERT MILTON CONGDON
MAY 26, 1936-MAY 15, 2021

WHEN THE LAST HAND COMES ABOARD

"No more a Watch to stand, Old Sailor,
You are outward bound on an ebbing tide.
Eight Bells has rung, and the last Watch done,
Now a new Berth waits for you on the other side

Your Ship is anchored in God's Harbor.
And your Shipmates, sailors of the Lord,
Are Mustered on deck to greet you,
And pipe you as you come aboard.

Her boilers with a full head of steam,
Cargo stowed, and Galley stored,
Just waiting to get underway,
When the last Hand comes aboard.

Look sharp! That Hand is you, Old Sailor.
And you'll be sailing out on Heavenly Seas.
May the wind be ever at your back,
Fairweather and God speed!"

—Richard John Scarr, England

"He will wipe every tear from their eyes. There will be no more death or mourning or crying or pain, for the old order of things has passed away…I am making everything new!"
—Revelation 21:4-5 (NIV)

"Those who sow with tears will reap with songs of joy. Those go out weeping, carrying seed to sow, will return with songs of joy, carrying sheaves with them."
—Psalm 126:5-6 (NIV)

"For your Maker is your husband—the Lord Almighty is his name—the Holy One of Israel is your Redeemer; he is called the God of all the earth."
—Isaiah 54:5 (NIV)

MY LAST ENTRY

OCTOBER 15TH

Five months passed giving me time to reflect. Tenderly, I still have tears as I share the last editing of my story. They are shed from a new perspective now. The Holy Spirit has slowly brought me to stop looking back and begin to look forward. You see, as I mentioned, my new assignment is just beginning. We move from faith to faith in our walk with the Lord. Never do we stop changing. If my story has moved you in any way, I encourage you to next pick up *The Astonishing Joy Novella* paperback on Amazon, to step into the power of the Father's Spirit. As I said earlier, place your Trust in God every moment! Seek him above all else. His Spirit will pour out incredible comfort to help you make a shift. You will become a lover of Jesus just as I am. You are His Treasure. You are a part of His Kingdom Royal Family. He loves you more in a moment than anyone could love you in a lifetime. May my story encourage you when and if you are ever facing the loss of a beloved. Make the moments count. Do not walk in denial of how important it is to help your beloved prepare for their time of being Called Home.

"So above all, constantly seek God's Kingdom and His Righteousness, then all these less important things will be given to you abundantly."
—Matthew 6:33 (TPT)

"Praise be to the God and Father of our Lord Jesus Christ the Father of compassion and the God of all comfort, who comforts us in all our troubles, so that we can comfort those in any trouble with the comfort we ourselves receive from God."
—2 Corinthians 1:3-4 (NIV)

RESOURCES

Goll, James. "Mentoring with James Goll Series" presented by Empower 2000 Kingdom Based Webinars, Fall 2021. Day 2

Kasyanenko, Steven, AKA, Steven K, Entrepreneur and Founder of Cast Your Net, Empowering Christians Platform, Sabbath Sermon 2/27/21, Prayers with Pastor Brenda Armstead, Day 7

RCP Intercessory Prayer for Apostle Guenther Hess, Pastor Stephen Guarneous and Rolland Abraham, Day 20

A SPECIAL TRIBUTE TO MY PARENTS

FRANK AND AGNES JURENKA

I want to take this opportunity to honor and bless you for your character and virtuous deeds throughout your life. I honor you for the years of selfless service spent in raising my brother Frank and I, for providing for our material, emotional, and spiritual needs. I honor you for preferring our needs over your own and for the sacrifices you made for our sake.

My beautiful parents met at a barn dance. I recall my mother showing me this barn and exactly how it all happened. As I look back and reflect about those times of my growing up in Holyrood, I could cry. So precious and orderly was my life. What a blessing to live in trust. I was always protected, loved, and cherished in this small Czech farming community forged by early Kansas pioneers.

My parents were quiet and faithful to their simple life. If I walked out to the street and looked down several blocks, I would see wheat waving in the fields. My mother and father were married in 1930. Dad worked in the oilfields and Mom managed our home and all things from her kitchen! Imagine that we never locked our doors except one time when we went on vacation to see Mount Rushmore.

Dad and Mom took my brother and me to church every Sunday. Dad made his family a priority. We had dinner together every night. We had gardens, chickens, and chores. I remember when milk was delivered in glass jars. We had large family gatherings on both my mother and my father's side of the family. That's just what families did to stay unified and in support of each other.

I grew up listening to the radio. In 1956 we got our first TV. My brother, Frank, who is 5 years older was smart and clever. I could write another book about his antics with his buddies.

My parents were very humble and would help our neighbors. These values were observed not instructed. You see, the small town took care of its own. My brother and I knew Dad's rules were firm. I honor and bless you Mother and Dad in heaven for helping me have your values to guide my life. I commit to carry forward your legacy of service and pass on your spiritual heritage to my child, Abby.

All My Love, *Dianne*

DIANNE CONGDON

Growing up in the '40s and '50s in the small Kansas farming town of Holyrood gave Dianne a foundation of trust and Christian "Love Your Neighbor" values. The quiet kindness of her parents, Frank, and Agnes Jurenka, led her to serve others at a young age. Dianne is a lover of Yeshua/Jesus. He came to her first through the rose wallpaper of her room when she was a little girl. Eye-level, this single rose became the flower that blossomed her into joyous expression. Today, she exists to serve by igniting joy in others.

Born Again at age 75, Dianne, now 80, shows us it is never too late to come to the Lord. You will find great inspiration in her other book, *The Astonishing Joy Novella* found on Amazon. She will open the door for the Holy Spirit with these newly released novellas. Dianne lives in Ft. Lauderdale, Florida. Her husband, Bob, was Called Home on May 15th, 2021. They have, between them, three children. *The Called Home Novella* reveals her days of tears which will warm your heart.

Find her on Facebook at Youthful Aging Lifestyle and her personal site. Dianne would love to meet you. She offers webinars and prayer support groups led by the Holy Spirit. She can be reached at www. ignitejoytoday.com Facebook: Youthful Aging Lifestyle for Spiritual Insight and Inspiration, and LinkedIn.com: Dianne Congdon, Kingdom Ambassador, Ft. Lauderdale, FL

ABOUT "LIVING WATER" ARTIST
CAROL CARTER

www.carol-carter.com

Carol Carter is an internationally renowned American artist whose work has been exhibited in six countries and published worldwide. She has won numerous international prizes for her work.

Carol received her MFA from Washington University, St. Louis. Awarded a MAA-NEA Fellowship in Painting and Works on Paper in 1994, she was voted Best St. Louis Artist by the Riverfront Times in 2000.

Carol has been published in many magazines and books internationally. She has taught in France, Norway, Ecuador, Hong Kong, and the US Virgin Islands. She teaches watercolor from coast to coast in the United States.

Among her many accolades, Carol received the Woman in Arts Recognition Award from the National Society of Daughters of American Revolution 2021.

Her work is represented in many public and private art collections.

"So be very careful how you live, not being like those with no understanding, but live honorably with true wisdom, for we are living in evil times. Take full advantage of every day as you spend your life for his purposes."

—Ephesians 5:15-16 (TPT)

"The LORD bless you and keep you;
The LORD make His face shine upon you,
And be gracious to you;
The LORD lift up His countenance upon you,
And give you peace."

—Numbers 6:24-26

ABIDING in JOY,

Dianne